The Unravelled Heart

A Journey of Breaking to Mending, Surviving to Loving, and
the Courage to Rise from Our Darkest Places, Undefeated.

KATHY PARKER

BALBOA.
PRESS
A DIVISION OF HAY HOUSE

Balboa Press books may be ordered through
booksellers or by contacting:

Balboa Press
A Division of Hay House
1663 Liberty Drive
Bloomington, IN 47403
www.balboapress.com.au
1 (877) 407-4847

Because of the dynamic nature of the Internet, any web addresses or
links contained in this book may have changed since publication and
may no longer be valid. The views expressed in this work are solely those
of the author and do not necessarily reflect the views of the publisher,
and the publisher hereby disclaims any responsibility for them.

The author of this book does not dispense medical advice or prescribe
the use of any technique as a form of treatment for physical, emotional,
or medical problems without the advice of a physician, either directly
or indirectly. The intent of the author is only to offer information
of a general nature to help you in your quest for emotional and
spiritual well-being. In the event you use any of the information in
this book for yourself, which is your constitutional right, the author
and the publisher assume no responsibility for your actions.

Any people depicted in stock imagery provided by Thinkstock are
models, and such images are being used for illustrative purposes only.
Certain stock imagery © Thinkstock.

Print information available on the last page.

ISBN: 978-1-5043-1097-0 (sc)
ISBN: 978-1-5043-1096-3 (e)

Balboa Press rev. date: 10/19/2017

Table of Contents

On Beginning to Mend

On Learning to Love Again

On Finding the Courage to Rise

Introduction

When I was younger, I was made of words: the books I read and the poems I wrote a comfort in the chaos that surrounded me. The words, though threadbare at times, made sense when little else did; they were air to my lungs, fire to my soul, and the only way I learned how to truly feel.

As I got older, I became aware I was different than those around me. I was ashamed of this broken girl with her misfit heart who was both too much yet nowhere near enough. I had no idea who I wanted to be; I simply knew the only way to be accepted was to conform. I placed all my words in a box and tucked them away on a shelf with other parts of myself I believed to be unacceptable. They wouldn't be needed anymore.

It would be many years before I would begin to unravel, but when I did, it would be a tempestuous tide of self-destruction that would take out everyone in its path, my wake littered with years of trauma, abuse, betrayal, shame, pain, and grief I could no longer hold within my worn act of perfectionism.

After years of pretending I had it together, I finally fell apart and was left standing at the ground zero of my life, surrounded by my own destruction. There was nothing more I could do but find the courage, strength, and determination to rebuild with what was left.

I would soon come to understand it was the best thing that could have happened to me.

My healing came through writing. It was there I remembered who I was and there I came together again, piece by piece and word by word. I pulled the box down from the shelf and dusted it off. Inside, I found the heart I had forsaken so many years earlier. It was a little neglected; a little war-torn. But still, it was beating.

These pages are a reflection of the journey back to myself; my sacred pilgrimage. They are words that have both broken and healed me. They are words that have saved me.

My prayer is they will do the same for you.

With love,

Kathy

For those whose hearts have come undone.

On Breaking
Wide Open

The Unravelling

She stands before the mirror,
Skinny limbs and tangled hair.
"Am I beautiful?" she wonders.
But already she knows that if
She were beautiful, then those
She loved wouldn't have left.
Instead, she knows her worth
Exists only between her legs.
She learns this from the men
Who steal in her room at night,
As the world is lost to slumber
And bottles of cheap red wine.

She stands before the mirror,
Blue suitcase and black eyes.
There is no beauty in bruises,
And no use for girls who can
No longer keep their mouths
Closed and their legs open.
She is city streets and pavers,

Desperate for a scrap of love.
They tell her she is beautiful,
And she gives them her body
Even though she knows they
Will forget her by tomorrow.

She stands before the mirror,
Painted face and perfect hair.
She pretends she is beautiful,
As if there is no scarlet letter
Seared upon her unclean skin.
She has learned love is given
To people who look beautiful,
Even if they are rotting inside.
And so she performs dress-ups
In a world she doesn't belong,
And hopes nobody can smell
The stench of her putrid flesh.

She stands before the mirror,
Bloodied hands and lost soul,
Shattered pieces that remain
From trails of self-destruction.
She is a heart torn, unravelled,

Trying to put herself together.
She is both broken and brave,
Still wondering if she will ever
Be beautiful, if she'll be worth
More than just her naked skin.
Still she gazes upon the mirror
And notices the fire in her eyes.

Love Can Look a Lot Like Abuse

And you once loved a boy

Who slit open your wrists

With his razor-blade tongue,

While you apologized to him

For blood stains on the floor

And thanked him for the way

He stitched up your wounds.

With rusted barbed wire thread.

As if love was ever meant

To feel like shredded skin.

As if love was ever meant

To feel like abuse.

Stained Fingerprints

How many layers of skin
Will I need to shed before
Your fingerprints no more
Are seared into my DNA?
For I've scoured my body
Of its recollection of you—
Sandpaper against flesh,
Raw skin torn to shreds.
But still I am covered in
Nicotine and grease and
Oil and filth and shame.
Still my undressed body
Remains nothing more
Than a place men occupy
To serve their misogyny.
They look both ways as
They walk out the door,
And I am left in silence
To try and wash clean
The stains they leave
Behind.

Raven

Like a raven,

He picks the flesh from your bones,

And you allow his shallow mouth

To feast upon your body

In the hope he will stumble upon your soul.

Dear woman, it takes more than a scavenger

To unearth the incomparable richness

That lies beneath your skin.

Nicotine Love

Your words are cigarette burns upon my skin;
They smoulder deep inside my weakened flesh.
I am incinerated bones and a blackened heart.
You bandage my wounds with your tepid sorry
Until you no longer see how much I still bleed.
Then you hold another cigarette to your mouth
And wait for me to light it.

Keep the Heart You Broke;
I'll Find a New One

I thought I would want my heart back. The one I gave to you.

After all, it belonged to me and contained everything I ever was.

My past—with all its mistakes, regrets, and ugly scars I had hoped you would learn to love anyway, for they were still a part of me, a part of my story.

My present—the way I laugh even when I hurt, the way I love even when I break, the way I choose to believe the best and fight for what is good and face each morning with courage, even when the night captures me with fear.

My future—where the best parts of me await my arrival, where all that I dream for, hope for, strive for will finally come together with surreal promise.

My heart belonged to me, but in freedom I gave it to you.

You knew of its fragility, its damage; how fiercely I protected it, guarded it, never allowed anyone close enough to hurt it again.

But you said you were different, you were safe.

So I offered it to you and trusted you to look after it as carefully as I always had.

At first you did. You admired my heart, held it with heedful hands, looked upon it with tender eyes. It

10

flourished in the warmth of your love, so consuming, so fervid.

But soon your gentle hold became a weight that crushed as the grip of your fingers pressed tighter around the heart you once held gently against your own chest.

Possession. Jealousy. Expectation. Demand. Control. Anger. Isolation. Abuse.

My heart was no longer beautiful to you, but an object you sought to destroy. You pressed it between your hands until I gasped for air, until I begged for you to let me breathe, but even then you didn't stop. You couldn't stop until you knew you had crucified me.

And then you left and took the last of my heart—shattered pieces no longer recognizable even to me, fragments of the woman I once was before you.

Still now, I lay upon the floor with my chest wide open, a gaping cavity where my beating heart once lived and breathed and thrived.

I thought I would want my heart back. The one I gave to you.

After all, it belonged to me.

But it's no longer the same heart.

It will always be different now because of you. It will never look the same, never feel the same, never fit the same as it once did inside my chest.

It will have traces of you left upon it, fingerprints burned into places you gripped with such merciless intention, cruel words seared into wounded flesh, memories that blacken the core where there had once been light.

No, I no longer want my heart back, the one that you destroyed. Pocket it; keep it as a souvenir to add to your collection of hearts you have left ravaged in your trail of desolation.

For I will find a new heart.

One that will be bright and shiny and whole.

One that will be wiser, less eager to trust, more cautious to love.

One that will know its worth and will only show itself to those who also know its worth, value, uniqueness, rareness, intention, beauty.

Yes, I will find a new heart.

A heart that, most important, will no longer hold any traces of you.

Until All That Remains

My heart lies exposed outside my broken chest.

It rests in the place where you ripped it out.

I'm not sure if it beats or merely bleeds,

But still it weeps at the mercy of your tongue,

At your words that tore through my flesh.

With careful hands, I bandage the wounds,

Then wipe clean the fingerprints you left behind

Before I place it back inside my chest.

In time, my damaged flesh will heal,

But the same poison that drips from your tongue

Will eat away at your corrupted soul

Until all that remains of you

Is the smell of regret

That seeps from your bones

As they rot beneath your festered skin.

And even if there was a way to pull stars down

And use them to seal the gaping holes inside our chests,

Still, infinite skies would never be enough

To fill the hollow spaces

Lost to misguided hands

And nonchalant hearts.

These Beautiful Scars

And even after
I'd sanded back layers of my skin
Until traces of your fingerprints
Remained no more,
And the raw ache of my flesh
Seeped blood upon the pages
Of the stories we never told,
Still the lines you drew upon me
Had settled in my core
And carved into my bones,
Until my body knew your imprint
More than it knew my own.
And it wasn't until I lost
All remnants of me,
In trying to scrub away
All remnants of you,
That I came to understand
Your fingers were knives,
And I had fallen in love
With these beautiful scars.

Collapsed Fortresses

And sometimes our fortress is really nothing more

Than a house of cards that collapses at the mercy

Of a single moment we never saw coming.

Fault Lines Upon Your Heart

"You're safe with me," you say
As I gaze at fault lines
Mapped upon your heart.
Desperate to believe you,
I pretend not to see
And look away.

"I love you," you whisper,
And I unpack worn bags
And make you my home,
Not yet wise enough to know
Your love would always come
At a cost.

I tiptoe around the cracks
Of our distorted foundations
And try not to notice the
Tremors that rattle my bones
As you kiss weak excuses
Upon my lips.

The walls close in around us,
I suffocate under the weight
Of their intimidating stare.
They scorn their judgement
Except, the walls are you,
Held by mistrust.

The air seeps with tension
As cold as your touch,
Even though hot anger
Simmers fire in your veins.
Tectonic plates shift, and rage
Pours onto me.

"Who is he?" you ask.
You never did understand,
For there is no other.
But you erupt, violent,
The furious earthquake
That destroys us.

Bridges Made of Arrows

And you talk of losing me

Like it was a choice I made, when every arrow

You used to pierce my heart

Built the bridge that led me away from you

And to the safe refuge of me.

1.42am

You found me in the deep,

My infinite soul untamed

Amongst wild oceans.

I called to you, beckoned you

Beyond comfortable shores.

"Shh," you hushed my heart.

"Come with me to the shallows,

For there we will not drown."

I took your hand and followed

To the place you felt safe.

The place I felt alone.

Ankle deep, we barely tasted

Salt upon our skin.

Here, you were content

While I gazed upon ink-blue water

And yearned to immerse myself

Within its weather-beaten waves.

"Come with me," I whispered

Against the warmth of your flesh.

"Come deeper, for there we will feel

Our passions, our emotions, our fire.

Come deeper, and let our souls discover

These unchartered waters together."

But you did not move, did not follow

As I stepped towards the horizon.

Instead, you stayed, skin deep.

I dove into the cool water,

Surfaced, glanced back.

You were no longer there.

And in that moment, I knew

You were not afraid of the deep

Because you didn't know how to swim,

But because you didn't know how to feel.

Imprisoned

And sometimes I wonder

    If our hearts will ever be heard

        Over the echo of ghosts that cry out

    From the graves inside

Our sorrowful chests.

Today I Missed My Train

Today, I missed my train
Because someone on the
Street reminded me of you.
Except, it wasn't really you,
And my heart tumbled out
My chest and slid through
The cracks in my ribs and
Fell onto the ground, where
I left it next to fallen leaves
And cigarette butts stained
With faded red-wine lipstick.
I wondered what I would do
If we did cross in the street.
Would I tell you of the times
I never called but almost did?
Or of the way your name was
Carved in every bottle I drank
And upon every word I wrote?
Or would I walk the other way
To make it to the train on time,

And hope your feet falter over

A lonely heart upon the street,

And you place it in your chest

And keep it safe until the time

I'm brave enough to knock at

Your door and ask for it back.

Apple Trees and Faded Dreams

As summer became lost to the faded light of autumn,

We ate apples from trees poisoned with resentment

And wondered how we too became lost

To the bitter words that fell from our tongues.

At Least They Keep Me Company

And at times I am so tired
From carrying the weight
Of the ghosts I once loved
In the shadows of my chest.
At night they keep me awake
With the rattle of their bones
Against the cages of my ribs.
I long to set them free of me,
To release my wearied heart
From the burden of their woes.
But when darkness surrounds,
And I have only the emptiness
To silence my unceasing fears,
I whisper to their wasted souls
That it is much less sorrowful
To spend my life haunted
Than alone.

Scraps of Love

You've been starved so long

That he feeds you crumbs from the table

And you thank him,

As if scraps of love will ever be enough

To fill the empty spaces

Inside your hollow bones.

Eyes of Hollow Caves

There is a girl in the mirror
With eyes of hollow caves.
She is tunnels of darkness
And tombstones of regret.
She is a cloaked graveyard
Of the people she has been,
Each with chameleon hearts
And a complaisant structure.
She has become a stranger
Buried beneath her ghosts.

And how many times do you
Have to live and die for them
In the hope they will love you
Before you can love yourself?

And Then You'll Remember How to Fly

And he will offer you words
Handpicked from his fields
Where manipulation grows
Upon soils rich with deceit.
They'll look like wildflowers
That smell like new promise.
And for a moment, your heart
Will be fooled by their beauty,
And your mind will then dwell
In places where luscious earth
Feels warm beneath your feet,
And the purple heather sways
In time to the summer breeze.
The places where wildflowers
Are born and freedom can be
Found under boundless skies.
And for a moment, you'll think
He actually means it this time.
Then you will look down upon
The marks around your ankles
And wrists that still weep tears
From shackles and chains that

He made you believe were love.
And then you'll remind yourself
That freedom doesn't look like
A cage, and love doesn't look
Like abuse, and once more
You will remember
How to fly.

When Love Isnt Enough

I know you love him, dear heart.

Love is enough, you tell yourself.

But deep in the hollow of places you don't want to explore, you know it isn't.

It used to be, back when it was whispered under summer skies with salty air in your lungs. When it was murmured beneath cherry trees that blossomed with the promise of harvest. When it was breathed against your neck as morning sun spilled golden light upon tangled sheets.

It used to be enough, back then—back when love was shiny and new.

But summer skies are soon defeated by dark-coloured clouds as cherry trees stand naked and forlorn in the starkness of winter and golden light recalls something beyond your grasp.

Love is enough, you tell yourself.

You know he loves you, even when he hurts you. He's sorry, always sorry. He wants to try harder, wants to do better, if you'll only give him another chance. You wipe away the tears that stream down his face. They are real tears, genuine tears, sincere tears, and you pull him close to you, forgive him, say you'll stay.

Love is enough, you tell yourself.

You believe in a love that can overcome, and you love harder. You love with all you have, all you are, all you can. You love until you are on the floor, until there are no more tears, until he has destroyed you to your bones. Even when there is nothing left of you, you love.

Love is enough, you tell yourself.

You wait for your love to sink into his skin, to spread through his cells, to seep into his bones and gush through his blood. You wait for your love to restore him, change him, stitch his broken pieces together. If you just love hard enough, he will understand love, he will love you better.

This is the power of the love you believe in, the love you give at any cost. The love you long so much to receive yourself.

Love is enough, you tell yourself.

Except when it isn't.

Because sometimes it just isn't.

It just isn't enough.

Sometimes, no matter how hard you love, it will never be enough.

It will never be enough to know respect, trust, commitment, loyalty, compassion, empathy, kindness, gentleness, support.

It will never be enough to overcome control, possessiveness, jealousy, manipulation, blame, guilt, neglect, anger, lies.

It will never be enough to restore what is broken, to make things right, to regain what has been lost, to cover all sins, to fill all gaps.

It will never be enough to make it worth the stay.

It will never be enough to withstand another day of abuse.

It will never be enough to make him love you with the love you deserve.

I know you love him, dear heart. I know you long for your happy ending. I know you wanted love to be enough. But you give your love away to one who does not understand it—one who does not deserve it.

The one most deserving of that love, dear heart, is you.

For you are a rare treasure, precious and irreplaceable. You are light to the darkest corners of humanity, rain upon parched fields, the warmth of flames under star-laden skies. You are calm rivers and wild oceans, breathless winds and hurricanes that rage, tropical nights by the sea and overcast days covered in blankets of fresh snow.

It's time to walk away. For when love destroys the sacred heart that beats inside your fragile chest, then love is no longer enough.

Don't settle for a love that does not see the incomparable beauty that is you.

Go now and love yourself with the love you deserve, the love you are entitled to.

Love yourself with the love he could never give you.

Love yourself so fiercely that you know without a

doubt the love you are worthy of, that you may never again settle for anything less.

Love yourself, because even though love isn't always enough, you, dear heart, always are.

You always will be.

On Barely
Surviving

To Darkness

Harsh winds began to rattle the windows
And the trees were stripped of their beauty,
And she mourned the final moments
Of autumn light as it became lost
To charcoal skies.
She shivered as the chill of winter
Settled under her skin.
It brought with it a heaviness,
As if each drop of rain that fell
Landed inside her hollow bones
And left her waterlogged; drowning
Beneath its bitter sadness.
She longed to stay above the darkness
That rose inside her chest,
But each day she grew colder
And apathy wrapped around her until
She surrendered to the weight of it.
"Just for a while I'll stay here
in this bleak comfort," she told herself.
"Just until the wind no longer howls
through my soul and the sky
lifts its sorrow from my eyes."

But it has been winter for so long now
That she fears she has become it, and
Her grief-soaked heart lies in silent hope
That one day someone will pull her
From the water and gently wring
The sadness from her bones.

Then there are those nights when you close the bathroom door and cry.

The nights when life hurts so much, your heart feels as though it's going to burst wide open and spatter the walls with bloodshed and tears.

Where you see your withered bones reflected in the pool of tears that has gathered on the cold tiles under your feet.

Where you wonder how you will ever find the strength to get off the bathroom floor.

But then you take a deep breath, pick yourself up, and wipe the tears away with the back of your hand.

You tuck your babies into bed, kiss them goodnight, and somehow fight through the pain that pulses through your veins and bleeds into your soul.

Because what else is there to do but continue on?

Life doesn't stop simply because your heart has shattered all over the bathroom floor.

And maybe this is what it means to be a warrior.

Maybe it's simply the courage we find to gather ourselves from the floor, wipe away the tears, and make it through another day.

And This Is How She Loves

And this is how she loves:

With one foot out the door,

Escape routes mapped upon

The paths of her weary veins.

She is tired eyes searching

For exit signs above doors,

Directions for the way out

Tattooed beneath her palms.

And always she keeps close

A suitcase by the front door,

For she no longer believes

In a love that could exist

Safe enough for her

To call home.

This Is Survival. Sometimes It Isn't Pretty

Sometimes survival looks beautiful. It is strength and courage and battle scars etched upon our skin for every war we have fought and won; battle scars that glisten in the sun as we stand upon mountaintops and look back at how far we have climbed along trails we never should have survived with the odds so damned against us.

But sometimes it isn't pretty.

Sometimes it's too much alcohol and words haemorrhaged on a page. It's 3 a.m. bloodshed and battle and demons slain. It's torrents of rage unleashed upon the things we remember even though we chose to forget. It's war fought in silence and tears, in fury and defeat. It's weeping and howling and desiring and longing and seething and wanting and healing and feeling.

It's rebellion against the deadness that blankets our soul.

It's anarchy against the numbness our hearts cannot escape.

It's not pretty.

But it's how we survive today, until we can survive better tomorrow.

The point is, we're surviving.

And sometimes that's all that really matters.

I hold tight but my fingers bleed,
Like that time you were insistent
You'd teach me guitar.
Do you remember I gave up then?
You told me it gets better, that the
Pain becomes worth it.
But I never was one to stick around
When things got hard; I never did
Know how to persevere.
Remember I told you once that I was
Not like an oak tree, with roots buried
Deep within the earth?
But I was the wilted leaves as they fell
Without colour or warmth, lost to the
Mercy of piercing gales.
You laughed and said my words were
So poetic, that I was such a dreamer,
A melancholy romantic.
Yet it is me carried away by icy winds,
While you still sit and play the guitar
Alone.

Haunted Houses

And beneath my skin lie the graves
Of past lives I have laid to rest.
But still the ghosts of my sorrows
Emerge from dust-filled crevices
And rattle the cages of my bones.
"Hush," I tell them, for I have
Been taught to fear my darkness,
To bury it with guilt, cover it with shame—
My corrupt flesh, my blemished soul.
Yet I cannot be afraid of the ghosts
That steal amidst my tombs of anguish.
Instead, their presence reminds me
We're all just haunted houses
Yet to understand
How frighteningly beautiful
We really are.

Tell Me, Can You Still Love Me Then?

But tell me,

Can you still love me

When the bitter winds

That rise from the south

Steal away the vivid colour

You have come to admire?

And I am left only bleak,

Grey, and stripped bare

Before your wondrous gaze?

But tell me,

Can you still love me

When I am without life

Under your warm hands,

When you dig far below

The outside of my skin

And stumble upon roots

Tangled, twisted, wayward

Between dark layers of my soul?

But tell me,

Can you still love me

When you find me there

At home in the darkness

Of my anguish and secrets,

Of my loneliness and rage,

When these unholy hands

Hold tight the black earth,

And I kiss both life and death?

But tell me,

Can you still love me

When there is just echo

Of the winter in my bones,

And I lay silent, unmoved

By your whisper upon me,

Instead lulled by the sound

Of gales that rush towards me

With their loneliness and despair?

But tell me,

Can you still love me

When the winds won't end,

And I am the barren hope

Of spring, kept out of reach.

When I am broken by winter

And too cold to speak words

Of how I need your love the most?

Tell me, can you still love me then?

And They Will Tell You How to Heal

And they will try to tell you how to heal.

Don't let them.

Their feet are not blistered from the
thousands of hard-fought miles

you have suffered.

Their knees do not bleed from the days
you have crawled through the dirt

when you could no longer walk.

Their bodies are not laced with scars
from the battles you have survived

time and time again.

Carry on, warrior.

You will heal.

Bur for today, broken has its own kind of beauty.

Winters Death

And there I found myself in the barren ground where you once stood,

Where I came to understand there must be winter—
Winter in all its loss, its grief, its letting go.
There must be a time for old things to die
So that new things may be born.

And No One Ever Told Me How to Break

And no one ever told me how
Healing was supposed to feel.
That it would be an anguish
That claws along my ribcage
Before it tears me wide open
And lays bare all my ugliness.
That it would be scarves of
Pain weaved around my neck
Like hands that grip my throat
And leave me fighting for life.
That it would be a wilted body,
Exhausted from the relentless
Fight against the demons that
Wage war upon my beaten soul.
That it would be bloody hands,
Blistered and raw from clinging
So tightly to the addictions that
Deaden this goddamn torment.
No, no one ever told me how
Healing was supposed to feel.

I didn't know it would hurt like
Barbed wire dragged over my skin
And knives gouged in my heart.
Yet all I know is before I'm able
To fully heal, I must allow myself
To fully break.

Broken Glass

But maybe none of us have ever been whole.

       Maybe we're all shards of broken glass,

Scattered,

   Trying to piece ourselves together.

Maybe some just find a way

       To smooth over the sharp edges

Before they cause another to bleed.

2am, Again

And they are so merciless,

These hours of darkness.

Broken clocks and silence

That shatters the windows

And shadows that arrange

Themselves in the hollows

Of my wretchedly sad mind.

There isn't anyone but me,

A small girl with a big world

That closes fast around her.

I am alone, lost, homesick.

A vagrant heart that beats

In hushed resonance with

The loneliness of the night.

I long to find my way home

So I tie my laces and follow

Trails of stale breadcrumbs

Back down the paths I have

Taken to find my way here.

But they are all overgrown

With weeds of remorse and

They only incline me further

Away from myself and I have
Lost the path that leads me
Narrowly back to my heart.
I ask the stars if they would
Show me the way, but they
Busily cavort with the moon,
Eager to skite their radiance
Before morning light steals
Away their glory, and I walk,
Alone, lost to the night again,
Still trying to find my way home.

It wasn't your fault.

It wasn't your fault nobody protected you from getting hurt when you were younger.

It wasn't your fault nobody told you how much you mattered, how much you were worth.

It wasn't your fault that you had no voice, that you were powerless and not taught to say no.

It wasn't your fault you didn't know how to draw the line around your heart, mind, and body to protect yourself from being hurt by others.

It wasn't your fault the people who should have shown you where to draw that line instead made you feel you weren't important enough to keep safe.

You grew up with no lines and no boundaries, and you didn't know the difference between love and abuse. Because of that, you allowed others to hurt you, when all you really wanted was for others to love you.

And that isn't your fault.

Let yourself be angry. Let yourself be angry that you were never told how much you were worth. That you never protected yourself because nobody ever protected you. That you allowed people to violate the lines that should have been there but never were because you weren't told how to put those lines in place.

Because you weren't told how important you were, and how much it mattered.

How much *you* mattered.

Let the anger rise within you. Allow yourself to cry tears of rage and grief for all you have lost. For all others have taken from you—not what you have given away, but what others have taken from you that you can no longer get back.

Use that anger to fight for yourself in the way you should have been fought for. Use it to reclaim all that has been taken, to reclaim your heart. Let the anger become a fire that rages in your soul and burns away the tarnish that others have left upon you. Let the flames consume you, let them purify you, let them cleanse you and refine you until all that is left is the beauty of who you really are.

Your worth is great. You were created by the same hands that created the galaxies and the stars and the oceans and the storms and the winds that rage across the four corners of the earth. You were breathed into existence not by accident, but with purpose, with promise. The entire universe listens just to hear the beating of your heart and the whisper of your breath. You were meant to be here. You were supposed to be here.

You were wanted here.

And you are worthy of the kind of love that nurtures your soul and heals your heart. A love that sees your value and worth and believes in you. A love that is strong and kind, loyal and true. A love that brushes the hair from your eyes, and kisses your forehead, and gives you its jacket when you are cold, and holds your hand when you are scared, and draws you into its arms and doesn't let go until it stops hurting. You are worthy of someone whose feet are anchored, who loves you when you radiate with the light of the moon and stars, and who loves you even harder when you are cast in the shadow of your own cold sorrow.

You are worthy of a love that will never, ever hurt you.

Draw your lines, dear woman, for within these lines lies the truth of all that you are worth.

And the moment you come to know this truth is the moment nobody can ever take that away from you again.

And Maybe I Will Go to Therapy

One day I will not be so young
And foolish in the ways I hurt.
I will arrive at therapy sessions
And learn how grown-ups heal.
I will take notes in a notebook
With its pages still untouched.

I will no longer soak my pores
With bottles of cheap red wine
Until I cannot tell the difference
Between alcohol and the blood
That seeps between the pages
Of the books I will never write.

I will no longer be the angry glow
Of cigarettes along empty streets
As I watch garbage trucks at 4 a.m.
And hold nicotine against my lips
And pretend it is you I hold there
While a streetlight flickers above.

I will no longer throw my outrage
Against the wall above your head
And watch as your fingers bleed
From sweeping shattered pieces
Into bins already full of confusion
That I cannot find a way to empty.

I will no longer fill your suitcase
With the heaviness of my fears,
Then show you to the front door.
Instead, I will tell you not to leave.
"I need you," I'll speak out loud,
And my eyes will not look away.

One day I will not be so young
And foolish in the ways I hurt.
And maybe I will go to therapy
And learn how grown-ups heal.
Or maybe there is no right way
To put ourselves back together
After all.

Fury

You are afraid of your own truth,
Too scared to believe in yourself
Because you have been made to
Believe you are stitched together
Wrong.

So you betray your soul through
The barren silence of your mouth,
Fearful if you raise up your voice,
You'll shatter the world with your
Fury.

We met before the time I knew myself.

It was the time when your approval mattered—when your approval became the foundation of the fragmented woman I was.

"You tell me who I am," I would say, as I awaited your instruction, wide-eyed and so very eager to please. And you told me who I needed to be to win your approval, and your love so laced with conditions and strings attached to heights I would never reach. You drew your lines and wooed me into them.

But your lines soon grew into walls. Walls so wide and tall and deep I could no longer see over them or around them. They closed in around me, and I became captive to them as they seethed with your hushed expectations.

I could never leave, for if I did I would know of your rejection, your disapproval, your criticism and abuse. And you were the one to build me, so I could not bear that you would break me.

Though afraid of the darkness, I stayed in your walls so fraught with conditional love and approval. Sometimes I would see a shard of light, fleetingly, and I would believe for one whimsical moment in the love you were never capable of; perhaps you would see beyond the surface so smeared with scars and recognize the purity of the heart underneath.

But I would soon learn your love was not light, nor hope, nor truth, nor freedom. It was the sound of the door as it closed behind you, the lock and key to your walls of darkness. I moulded and shaped and bent myself to fit within your walls, but no matter how small I became for you, my efforts were futile when the walls would always change shape on your irrational whims.

The darkness grew thicker, more pungent with your dissatisfaction, until my heart too became dark, filled with a blackness that poisoned my mind and wasted away my soul. I began to hate myself almost as much as you did, this girl who could do no right. Worthless, hopeless, useless.

You nearly broke me.

But not quite.

Because you didn't hear the primal roar that began to swell inside the pit of my stomach before it made its way into my bones and out through my scream. You didn't know what I had already survived through, the tenacity of my strength, my courage, my resilience. You didn't know of my fighting spirit that may have lay down short of hope for a time, but never without defeat.

For I cannot be defeated.

I am a warrior, made of the dust and the stars and the oceans and the skies.

I am a phoenix that has risen once again, a force of nature, a hurricane, a storm, a raging fire.

I am certain, I am sure. I am complete.

My feet stand firm upon the earth and she carries

me, her energy rising up within me, and though the winds may blow, I cannot be moved. The shard of light was never you. It was always the light within me, the embers of a powerful spirit you never quite burned out.

Your walls have no hold on me as I walk away now, light on the wings of my freedom. You tried, but you did not break me. You will try again; you always do. But I refuse. I know who I am now. I hear the voice of truth as it whispers in the stillness of the place you used to be. My light can no longer be contained.

And I know I will never again be found captive within the dark walls of your approval.

On Beginning
to Mend

This Is How You Mend Your Broken

And today you picked yourself up from the floor

And made it through another day.

Never let anyone tell you what your
brave should look like.

This is how you heal:

One hard-fought day at a time.

This is how you mend your broken.

Survival

And sometimes it is so hard to care for others when you can barely care for yourself. When you are tired in a way sleep will never ease. When the night goes too long and the morning comes too soon and you wonder where you will draw the strength to get through another day when there is nothing left in your drought-stricken bones.

You dress, make coffee, force a smile and hope nobody studies your eyes close enough to see the 4am loneliness that still lingers like tendrils of ivy that have crept in and wrapped themselves around your soul; relentless, incessant, determined.

You wear brave so well that nobody sees beyond the surface of your survival to the battle beneath. The way every day is another day on the frontline, no matter how exhausted and torn apart you already are. Nobody sees the fresh blood drawn from old wounds or the anguish in your muscles that are always on guard or how much it takes for you to get back up when your knees bleed from the crawl.

You do the best you can but it never feels enough. Every night inadequacy whispers its shame against your ear and soon your heart beats in time with its words. *Failure. Disappointment. Hopeless. Weak. Useless. Incapable.* All you ever wanted was to do better – to be better – than what was shown to you. But you feel as though you fall so short. That you let down those who need you. That you aren't enough and never will be.

You're so damned hard on yourself. As if it isn't enough just to have survived this far. As if it isn't enough to have found a way to stitch your broken pieces together when there was such little of yourself left. Instead, you're so ashamed of not being straight lines and seamless joins and all you see are the jagged scars drawn across your body and your fingers trace over them like braille and to you they spell defeat.

Darling, let me tattoo truth inside your wrists so when you've forgotten who you are you need only look down.

Undefeated. Worthy. Resilient. Strong.
Courageous. Determined. Perfect. Enough.

And if the light grows weak and the words fade before your eyes I will say them out loud and the letters will fall from my mouth and form a bridge that will lead you back to yourself once more.

You are so much more than you see. Your weakness intertwines with courage, your fear entangles bravery and your vulnerability is laced with strength. There is so much fortitude in the way you give all you have, even when you have nothing to give.

I know, today, you don't believe me. I know today you are tired eyes and tear-stained pillows and battle scars etched upon your face. But all I ask is you look away from what you have come to believe about yourself and

67

instead, look at me. Search my eyes for your reflection and in them you will see the truth.

That the way survival looks on you, my love, is nothing short of breathtaking.

The Path of the Survivor

There is a path we take.

It is not a journey forward, but one that leads us back.

Back to the places we were first broken.

Back to the places we fear the most.

We resist it, fight it.

But on that path lies a trail of broken pieces. Splintered fragments of ourselves we left behind when they were too sharp to hold and cut us open. Back then, we didn't know how to stop the bleeding. So we left the pieces scattered on the path and continued on our journey.

Removed from the pain, but separated from ourselves.

But now, we must go back for those pieces.

For this is how we put ourselves back together.

This is how we become whole.

We gather the pieces we abandoned and place them inside us, where they always belonged.

Find courage, dear one, and tread upon the path. Pick up the broken pieces and hold them close. Remember the way they once cut your hands yet no longer do, for now your hands are stronger and your skin is thicker, and though scarred you no longer bleed.

Feel the weight of the pieces in your hands and notice

you are strong enough to carry that weight now. Turn them over, adjust them, move them, line them up. Make sense of them. Place them side by side. Repair them. Restore them. See the way they come together with cracks and lines and faults and imperfect edges that will never fit like they used to.

But see how they are once more made whole.

This is how broken things mend,

How broken people mend:

In flawed perfection.

It was never your fault you were so broken. It was never your fault you left so much of yourself behind. But now is the time to go back and pick up the pieces. Do not fear the path. You know the way; you have walked it before. It is your path. And these are your pieces. They belong to you. Pick them up, put them back together, and place them inside your chest. Allow them to make you whole again, as you were always meant to be.

Broken no more.

For this, dear one, is the path of the survivor.

Supernova

And darling,

I know it hurts to break wide open,

but you must remember

a supernova is only created

through the explosion of a star.

Galaxies are reborn through destruction.

You will be too, my love.

You had to grow up so fast, didn't you? You were so young when they handed you such a heavy box to carry. A box filled with secrets, lies, and shame. It contained the weight of the world, and your job was to protect it, to never put it down.

It was your responsibility, wasn't it? To keep everything hidden away in the box. While other children played in fallen leaves under autumn skies and laughed with gleeful abandon, you sat with your box and watched and longed and imagined the feel of grass under your feet. But you were so scared of what might happen if you put the box down, even for a moment, and so there you remained; too grown-up to play childish games. And at night when crickets chirred under skies mantled with glistening stars, even then you would lie awake, too afraid to fall asleep, too afraid that if you did, you would fail. This was your burden to carry: to be the keeper of secrets. It was up to you to keep the secrets safe.

As you grew, you hoped the box would become easier to hold. But over the years, you had shoved your own secrets into it—the abuse, the neglect, your lies, your manipulations, your deceits, the masks you wore, the things you did. Your box was laden with coping mechanisms needed for you to survive, but you didn't know that back then. It was your box of shame, and your weary body crushed under the weight of it.

Childhood passed; games and play and laughter

were forsaken for seriousness, solemnity, maturity. You were left to look after yourself, weren't you? You had to learn self-reliance when you were still so small. But you learned, didn't you? You learned to do it on your own, to not need anyone or anything. You learned to hold it together. Even when you wanted to cry, to scream, to fall apart. Even when you longed to surrender, to trust, to love, to be loved. Even then, you stayed strong and in control. You never let go of your self-sufficiency. You never let go of the box. You never fell apart. You did what you had to do.

But now your bones ache, and your muscles burn, and your hands shake from the cold. Your legs are weak under the weight of all you have carried. You are forlorn from years without laughter. Depleted from such little sleep. Withered from worry, from care, from strain.

Beautiful woman, lay down your box. It was never yours to carry. The secrets were never yours to keep. The shame was never yours to bear. The burdens were never to be carried upon your shoulders. Lay it down. Rest. Breathe. Whisper words of truth to the precious child within. Tell her she can let go now. Tell her she is safe. She is safe to find joy, to laugh, to play, to trust, to love, to be loved.

Lay down the box, beloved. It no longer serves you. Leave it behind and walk the new path that has been set before you. You are free.

You are free.

Refined into Gold

He wanted me to believe I was worthless.

But once his destructive fire had passed,

I saw it was my heart that had been refined into gold,

And his corrupted soul will forever be tarnished

By the heat of his own vindictive flames.

Foolish girl,

You turn away from the world because you believe the mistakes you have made are tattooed all over your body, and that is all the world can see: marks of shame you cannot wipe clean no matter how many years you scrub your skin, until no more blood can seep from your pores still stained with filth and sin.

You turn away from the world because you believe that you are defined by your past and the choices you made when there were no other choices, that you are bound to the girl you once were by the invisible ropes still tied around your hands and feet, held in place by words of shame that will never deliver you from their grasp.

You turn away from the world because you believe you do not deserve to hold your head high and look it in the eye, that you carry a scarlet letter upon your forehead that will blind those who dare to look your way, and you cannot stand to see the way they turn their faces from your tainted humanity.

You forget, foolish girl.

You forget what you have survived.

You forget you fought alone against the world when your hands were too small to defeat the weight of it, and so you took it on as your own even though it almost crushed you.

You forget you were betrayed by those who should have protected you, and so you barricaded yourself behind hard edges and sharp corners and promised to never trust or need another again.

You forget the way love was shown as abuse and abuse was shown as love, and the shame you were forced to carry because of the way you longed to be loved even when that looked like abuse.

You forget you sat alone in a room filled with despair as your hands shook and blood trailed down your wrist—and in that moment when you could have chosen death, you chose life.

You forget you have every reason to be hard, but you choose to remain soft. You have every reason to hate, but you choose to show mercy. You have every reason to cast judgement, but you choose to speak grace. You have every reason to fuck this world the way it has fucked you, but you choose to heal it instead.

You forget you have survived what most people never could.

Foolish girl, you are not foolish at all.

You are a warrior.

You are strength. You are bravery. You are courage. You are hope. You are light. You are truth. You are love. You are survival. You are kindness. You are wisdom. You are redemption. You are transformation. You are revolution.

And most of all, you are worthy to love and be loved.

You just need to believe it.

Dandelion Hearts

Your dandelion heart blows in the breeze,

Pieces scattered amongst all you meet

In the hope a seed will fall upon the one

Who longs to nurture your gentle soul.

Instead, the pieces land upon barren fields

And wither in the cracked, parched soil

Of shallow hearts and thoughtless hands.

Dear one, gather the seeds back to yourself;

They weren't made for those who trample

Their careless strides upon fragile birth.

Place them back inside your empty chest

Until once more your heart is complete

Until all you are set apart to be begins

To burst forth upon the rich earth

Of your glorious flesh and bones.

You Are Not Measured by How Short You Fall

I know how hard you try, precious one. I know you still carry the pain of the past, the pain over things you cannot take back, and I know how much that hurts. You long to make it right because that is your heart, it hurts you to hurt others. But in the time of your own hurt, the world spun out of control, and you were caught in the chaos. Now you look back at the destruction and weep for what is lost, for what you will never get back.

You are haunted by the voices of your sorrow, the ones that seek to remind you that you will never be more than your mistakes. But do not listen to these voices, for they lie to you.

You are not measured by how short you fall, but by how great you love.

It matters not what the world believes of you, for their judgement is fraught in the denial of their own humanity, their own need for grace.

Take your heavy heart to the water's edge and lay it down upon the shoreline where salty waves wash away the tarnish. Let your pain be carried out to sea, let it be held by the hands of creation, then leave it behind as you place your heart back inside your chest—now weightless, now free, once again filled with light.

Your heart is pure, true, and good. You are here because creation dreamed you into being; it longed for your presence in the world, your heart, mind and soul, and it gazes in awe at all you are.

You are worth more than you could possibly know. Your mistakes don't change that, and neither do your regrets, your brokenness, your weaknesses, your flaws.

The voices will always try to hold you captive to your past, to your shame. Pay them no heed.

Hear only the voice of truth.

For this is the voice that longs to set you free.

Reborn

And when you have lost
So many pieces of your heart
To careless hands,
And only faded particles remain,
Remember the most luminous stars
Have been created from dust.
You too will be reborn
And set fire to the night, my love.

You Are Enough

What would it look like if, just for today, you could believe you were enough?

If you could let go of the ways you believe you have failed and fallen short? If you could look beyond your flaws and mistakes and believe, just for today, they don't define you? If you could be as gentle on yourself as you are on others?

For no matter how many times you have fallen apart at the mercy of your own failings, you are still stitched together with good intentions. Your heart still seeks righteousness, goodness, compassion, mercy, love. You still search for light in the dark places of humanity. You still choose to believe the best when you have stood at the hands of the worst.

Precious one, you will always be enough. You don't believe it as tired eyes stare at the glow of moonlight on the ceiling night after night. Nor as the walls whisper your failings, and the wind howls your shame against windows that rattle into the very core of your existence. You don't believe you will ever be anything more than the trail of destruction you left in your wake, in the days when your heart hurt so badly in your chest that you became a tsunami as it approaches the shore, bound for decimation.

But you were chosen. You were set apart. You were sculpted by the hands of creation, fashioned into being by the very hands that created the oceans and the stars and the mountains and air you breathe into lungs that ache with burdens you carry on your chest.

You have never failed. There is never any failure in this journey, only opportunity to become stronger and wiser, to do better, to love harder.

You will never be perfect. But you were never meant to be.

You are jagged edges and unhealed wounds and a patchwork soul. You are human.

You are enough. You always have been, for that is the mystery of grace.

What would it look like if, just for today, you could believe it?

Freedom's Kiss

She finally let go of all that kept her
captive to her yesterdays,
and never before had the kiss of goodbye
tasted so much like freedom.

You Weren't Too Much for Him

You always felt you were too much for him, with your spirited heart and vibrant laugh, your reflective mind and unabashed emotion.

Him, who liked to keep things simple, uncomplicated. Nothing serious, nothing deep, nothing complex. Nothing that would make him think or feel.

Scared to frighten him away, you did what you always do.

You made yourself less.

Piece by piece, you tore off the parts of you that you thought would be more than he could handle. You lay them out thinly between pages of the tattered book you keep—the one that hides all the parts of yourself you've been afraid to show the world.

You made yourself more manageable, more palatable, easier to handle. Because if this is what it would take for him to accept you, want you, maybe one day even love you, then you would do it. It would be worth it, for him.

For a long time, you pretended you were happy. Maybe sometimes you even thought you were. But sometimes those torn-off parts called out to you, and your body ached to have them back, to be complete again. "No," you told them. "You are too much, you'll only frighten him away," as you pressed the pages together once more.

You tried to convince yourself you could survive this

way, as a silhouette—no substance, no soul. But you were empty, hollow, wasted away. Weightless, you struggled to hold yourself up any longer. You needed those parts of yourself back, the ones that held you together, the ones that made you whole.

And so, one piece at a time, you began to restore yourself. Slowly, quietly. Maybe he wouldn't notice. Or maybe if he did, he would somehow learn to love those extra parts of you anyway

The more complete you became, the harder it was to fight the truth of you. You began to share your mind, speak your thoughts. To laugh with abandon, to allow joy, sadness, anger, enthusiasm, fear, confidence and love to flow from you like water, like the tears he always told you not to cry. You embraced your imagination, passion, creativity, intellect, complexity, intuition, wild spirit, and ferocious heart.

You became who you were always meant to be.

And then he left.

You became too much.

You blamed yourself, as if you had done something wrong. If only you had stayed small, stayed less. If only you had kept those parts of yourself hidden like they had always been. If only you hadn't scared him away.

No, dear heart.

You weren't too much for him.

He was never enough for you.

You need more than a silly boy who scares easily.

A boy who is only willing to dip his toes in shallow water for fear of the deep. A boy who has no interest beyond the surface of your skin—to the beautiful enigma beneath.

You need a man with the heart of a warrior, brave and loyal, fearless and strong. Deep and passionate and as filled with the complexities of the universe as you are.

Maybe you will find him. Maybe you won't. Either way, it doesn't matter.

For he is not the hero of this story.

You are.

Because you are enough. And all you will ever need is within you.

Within your goddamn glorious, wondrous *too much*.

The Pioneer

He draws lines upon your body,

Maps out the places he has travelled,

Places where his hands

Have skimmed the surface of your skin.

The lines meet, join together,

And he thinks he knows you

By the fingerprints he leaves behind.

But your body has been travelled by many,

Offered to every sojourner

In the hope one will stay long enough

To stray from the well-worn roads of your flesh

To the unknown paths of your soul.

Dear heart,

You don't need a traveller

Who seeks a warm bed to spend the night

Before he continues on his way.

You need a goddamn pioneer

Who longs to unearth places in you not yet found,

Who is without fear of the tangled wilderness

He'll find beneath your skin,

Who prefers the uneven crags of your heart

And the deep murkiness of your soul.

An explorer

Who covers his hands in the dirt of your essence

And drips in the sweat of your being

Before he finds his way home,

Settled in the depth of your core

On the road he carved with his own two hands.

I No Longer Need You

I thought it would be painful, letting you go.

I thought I would suffer, that my heart would be anguished with the loss of you. Or worse, maybe it would stop beating altogether.

Maybe without you, I would simply cease to exist.

I thought I would become adrift, for you had been the anchor I had formed my identity upon, the compass I had relied on for my direction. I thought without you, I would become lost, disoriented.

I had expected to taste salty tears as they fell upon lips that once spoke so fondly of you; that my head would lay on my pillow damp with tears for as many nights as the moon continued to kiss the stars.

But one day, I just knew.

I hadn't expected such a feeling of relief as I cut the ropes that once shackled me to you. One instant of tremendous clarity. One instant where I finally knew.

I no longer needed you.

I no longer needed your opinion of me, your affirmation, your approval.

I no longer needed your judgements, your criticisms, your condemnations.

I no longer needed your expectations I could never meet, your hoops too high to jump through, your goal posts that shifted with every changing breeze.

I no longer needed your blame, your excuses, your justifications.

I no longer needed your pseudo love, fraught with conditions and attached with strings.

I thought I needed you. I didn't.

I thought it would be hard to let you go. It wasn't.

I thought I would miss you. I don't.

For in one instant, my heart was awakened to the truth of who I am.

I am more than the lies you made believe about myself. I am more than the look of failure in your eyes when I fell short of your demands. I am more than how worthless you made me feel. I am more than the ways you tried to break me.

I am a warrior, sculpted by the hands of creation, fashioned into being by the very hands that created the oceans and the stars and the mountains and air.

I am strong, I am brave, I am wise. I am gentle of spirit with the heart of a lioness.

I am creative, passionate, sensitive, and kind. I am of open heart and open mind. I am powerful, generous, thoughtful, daring, empathetic, raw, complex, courageous, understanding, forgiving.

I am everything you are not.

I will no longer carry the shame you made me suffer under the weight of.

That shame belongs to you.

And I will no longer carry my hate for you.

For that will only ever bind me to your darkness and give you permission to destroy my light. It will allow you to stay within me, to destroy my peace, to blacken my heart with the malice that lives within you.

It will tie me to your soul-destroying bitterness, your ugliness.

It will anchor me once more to you, who tried to drown me.

Instead, I will choose to go into the world and love more fiercely, show more compassion, be more generous, offer more kindness.

I will choose to forgive. For me, not for you.

I will choose to sow what I wish to see reaped for my children's future.

I will choose to disempower hate.

I will choose freedom.

I will choose love.

I will stand firm upon the unshakeable truth of who I am,

And I will soar to heights you will only ever dream of.

For I have let you go.

No longer am I held down by all I allowed you to be in my life.

I no longer need you.

Your Naked Soul Is Worth More Than Your Naked Body

You stand and gaze at your body reflected in the mirror before you.

The body you just gave away again, even though you knew.

You knew he wouldn't stay.

Your eyes follow the length of your collarbone to your shoulder, down your arm, the roundness of your breast, the subtle curve of your hip. The places where his fingers burned against you as he whispered futile promises upon the hungry needs of your neglected heart.

Yes, he saw your naked body.

But he cared not for your naked soul.

Yet you are bound to your ocean of maybes. Maybe if he craves your body, he will ache for your soul. Maybe if he traces lines upon your flesh, he will trace lines down the spine of your ambitions, fears, yearnings, and mysteries. Maybe if you give yourself away one last time, he will be the one to answer the question that has consumed your heart since you were a small girl who danced in a princess dress and a tiara—"Am I lovely?"

For this is what you burn for: To have your question answered. To know you are worth the time it would take for someone to learn your soul, and to fall in love with it. To know you have captivated another with your very being. To be cherished, valued, protected.

To feel, for the first time in your life, completely and utterly lovely.

But your question was never answered as you twirled in your princess dress, or as you clumsily paraded in high heels, or as you adorned your face with blue eye shadow and gaudy lipstick. It was never answered as you traded your dress-up world for your grown-up world, as you strived, excelled, and achieved in the hope you would be seen.

You were never told how lovely you really are. How much you are worth. And so you give yourself away in the hope he will answer your question. In the hope he will find you lovely. In the hope that, somehow, his fingerprints upon your skin will bridge together the abyss upon your heart.

But once again you are left alone, your naked body used to satiate the need of a silly boy who didn't care to see your naked soul.

If only you could see.

If only you could see how lovely you are. The way your eyes carry the glow of a thousand fireflies. How your laughter fills the spaces of a broken chorus.

The enchantment of your thoughts, delightfully articulated into words. Your heart, with all its intricacies and uncertainties, exquisite, rare, invaluable.

Maybe nobody ever told you.

But I'm telling you now.

You don't need to give yourself away to find the answer to your question.

The answer is already there, staring back at you.

You are lovely.

Lovelier than you will ever know. Worth more than you will ever know. More important than you will ever know.

Wait for the one who falls in love with your naked soul. The one whose eyes will gaze beyond your flesh and into the entirety of you. Wait for him, for he will memorize the quickening of your heartbeat, hold close the rhythm of your breath. He will hear your unspoken words, dust the hopes hidden in your dark corners, and trace his finger along the stories you keep beneath your bones.

Wait for him not because he is worth it.

But because you are.

Viking Funeral

Today I laid to rest your memory.

I placed it in a box of unfinished wood where
rough edges left splinters in my fingers, and
flakes of paint fell upon the empty spaces
in my hands you filled so long ago.

Along shorelines we'd roamed, I traced the echoes
of salt air that had once tasted like hope, until I
found where your promises had been scrawled
in the sand, now washed away by fickle tides.

I gave you a Viking funeral. Not because you
deserved one—no, darling, we both know you were
only ever a coward, a boy dressed in mans clothes.

No, I gave you a Viking funeral so I could set
your memory on fire and watch it burn, the way
you had stood and watched me burn for you.

But, darling, you didn't know I was made of gold.

Now it is you who lies amongst embers while I am
alight with the blaze of a thousand stars inside my soul.

No longer burning for you, but for me.

In the death of your memory, I am raised to life.

When I chose to let you go, there was no great moment of triumph.

There wasn't an earth-shattering epiphany that changed my life, where music played and the universe conspired to bring everything together for good.

There was no conflict, no turmoil, and no struggle. No internal argument. No weighing of pros and cons. No decision to be analysed to death—even by me, who cannot make a decision without weeks of obsessive thought over every possible outcome.

There were only two words, when I chose to let you go:

No more.

No more will I measure my worth against your opinion. No more will I be pressed into the shapes you carved for me. No more will I tell my heart to quiet down, ashamed of its clatter. No more will there be blood on my feet from the eggshells I walked on as I tried not to give cause for your disapproval.

No more will I anguish over the ways you misunderstood me. No more will I fight to justify the intention of my heart. No more will I beg for you to see me, the real me—to know me, to love me.

No more will I live my life for you.

When I chose to let you go, there was no holy encounter. The stars did not collapse from the sky and cascade into the oceans. There was no ferocious wind that rattled the walls or blazing fire that consumed all within its destructive path.

There was only quiet resolution, the silent death of leaves that drift to the ground as frost begins to waste them away.

And there I found myself, in the barren ground where you once stood; I came to understand there must be winter.

Winter in all its loss, its grief, its letting go.

There must be a time for old things to die, that new things may be born.

When I chose to let you go, it was for me.

I learned to love myself even when you made me feel I deserved no love. To honour my own needs, my own heart, and my own potential. To walk my own path, not yours. To not be pulled back into your confines while my spirit yearned to be free.

When I chose to let you go, I made coffee, ate toast, and folded clothes. I went to yoga and collected my mail and paid my bills. There was nothing out of place on the outside of my ordinary life—no visible change, nothing new or different.

There was only surrender. One moment. One breath.

I chose to let you go.

And in doing so, I chose me.

Names Carved in Flesh

Today, I stripped back my skin

And searched for the place

Where your name was once carved

Upon the rawness of my eager flesh.

You have fallen away from me—

Or have I fallen away from you?

Or maybe we are both misplaced,

Trapped beneath memories that collapsed

Under the weight of misunderstanding.

I needed to know if you were still there,

Below my skin where you used to live,

Where I had held you safe against my bones,

And you had held me safe against your chest.

But the letters of your name were gone,

Lost between the weather-worn gaps

Of the bridges we never made.

My flesh was blank, empty.

I was surprised to discover

I did not grieve the loss.

Neither did I feel the despair.

Instead, I wrote my own name

In the place your name once filled.

The letters aligned, side by side,

And I was breathless in their wake,

For I have never before noticed

The way they looked like freedom

And sounded like hope.

I laid my skin down once more

Upon the place you no longer exist,

And in the beauty of that moment,

I am filled with promise.

I am made new.

Stubborn Heart

Foolish heart, you had just started to heal.

But as I hold you in my hand, you once again bleed; old wounds torn open, new wounds raw and vivid against achromatic flesh.

I examine the damage. Once a pure canvas, you are now a war zone, disfigured by the stories you will never tell.

I count the bruises first, trace a finger along your scars, some more faded than others. My finger rests on the one from the first time you were hurt. It was always the deepest one, wasn't it? I don't need to look closely to know it still weeps, to know it never healed like you pretended it did.

You were so quick to forgive, to trust again.

You begged to lie upon my sleeve. I warned you against it, that it would make you too vulnerable, but you insisted. You believed in the hearts of others, in the goodness of them. You believed all hearts were the same as you.

You believed in love, because is that not what you were made for?

But you didn't know how cruel other hearts could be.

You were a soldier on the frontline, and you battled hard against the ones who tried to bring you down. Over and over I stitched your wounds until you were a patchwork heart, held together with little more than frayed thread and faltered hope. And yet on my sleeve you stayed, and you fought until there was too much blood and not enough thread, and I placed you back in my chest, determined to keep you safe.

But dear heart, you were so stubborn, and though I told you, "No more!" I could not keep you in my chest, so determined you were to prove me wrong. To prove the power of forgiveness, grace, second chances, unconditional love.

But you weren't healed. You weren't ready.

And this time, the wound struck too deep.

You couldn't get back up.

Now you lay limp in my hands, surrendered, defeated. I zigzag the thread through your wounds, pull them closed, hope my saltwater tears cleanse the place where his words plunged into your fragile core.

Precious heart, you have withered, paled, turned cold and stone-like. You no longer believe in love or in the goodness of other hearts.

But I will keep you safe in me, and you will heal. Soon, the bleeding will stop. Your wounds will become scars, and they will fade with time, reminders of how strong you really are. With each new day, I will hear the sound of your resolve as you beat harder against my chest.

Dear heart, I am proud of you. You are right to believe in love and to fight for it.

Don't allow the ugliness that resides in others take away the beauty in you.

The world is full of hearts like you. Kind hearts, merciful hearts, brave hearts, compassionate hearts, generous hearts, forgiving hearts, loving hearts.

And when you find them, you will know them.

For they too bear the scars of a warrior.

Foolish and determined, just like you, to believe that love can heal a broken world.

Beloved, Come Back to Yourself

This morning, you woke again and carried the weight of your sadness into your day. You wonder how you got here, to this place where you are so broken, so lost.

You no longer even know who this woman is, the one with the drawn face and colourless eyes. She is a stranger, a shell of emptiness and grief.

There is nothing left of you, only the parched skin that covers your withered bones. Somewhere within you a heart must still beat, but it is faint and thready, and you wonder how it even draws life when you have given so much of it away.

You never meant to lose so much of yourself. You thought maybe if you broke off pieces of your heart and placed them in the hands of others, they would see the gift you had given them. Maybe they would know how much it cost you to tear apart your flesh, and they would cherish this piece of you that rested in their hands. Maybe they would see you, know you.

Maybe they would love you.

Piece by piece, you ripped yourself apart. Piece by piece, you gave yourself away. Sometimes for a moment, sometimes for a night. Sometimes for a promise that fell from a hasty tongue onto the barren ground at your weary feet.

But never for the love you so craved.

But it didn't matter. You were desperate to be seen, to be loved, so you continued to give your heart away. Now your breath is weak and your chest is empty, and you can no longer feel the life force that once pulsed through your veins or the hope that once thrived in your soul.

You allowed the pieces of your heart to fall through the fingers of those who didn't know how much it was worth.

Because no-one ever told you how much you were worth.

But hearts as valuable as yours were never made for careless hands.

Beloved, come back to yourself.

Roam the earth, far and wide, and gather back the pieces you have lost. Bring them close, dust them off, and place them back inside your chest. Feel as you begin to mend. Watch the way your heart draws back together. Listen to its strength as it beats faster, the way it finds the song that has called your name since the moment you were born into existence.

Beloved, come back to yourself.

For your heart contains the mystery of the universe within its every breath. You are the ferocity of wild storms on a summer night, the whispered hush of the sun as it kisses the horizon. You are the thunder that rattles the windows of cities, the gentle harmonies that wash people clean with their tears. You are the fury of untamed oceans that lash against beaten shores, the softness of rain that lands silently upon fallen leaves. You are madness and chaos, passion and fire, stillness and calm—a beautiful contradiction that leaves the world breathless in your wake.

Beloved, come back to yourself.

No longer give your heart away to those who do not see the beauty that lies within their hands.

Love your own heart with every measure of the love it deserves so that you will never again settle for a love less than everything you have ever been worth.

Veil of Shame

Dear woman,

Pick up your heavy burdens.

You have dwelled long enough

Within your spaces of regret

And your shadows of remorse.

Take off your clothes of mourning,

Remove the veil from your eyes,

And run barefoot through

Fields awash with gold.

Call out to the wind;

Tell her to blow to the

Corners of the world,

Gather all that is yours

And bring it back

To where it belongs.

All you have lost,

All you have given away,

All you have sacrificed,

All you have traded

In the name of the

Love you cast away

To drought-stricken hearts.

Feel it sweep upon you,

Rush through your wild hair,

Fall onto hungry skin

Until all the stars in the galaxies

Filter through famished bones,

Soak into hollow lungs,

And the particles of the universe

Are again held inside your heartbeat.

Then revel in your untamed beauty

And set the world afire with your glory,

For your soul was not made to be hidden

Underneath a veil of shame

That was never yours to wear.

I Forgive You, and in Doing So, Forgive Me

Today, I woke with your name upon my tongue, bitter like the dregs of whisky that burned my throat last night as I drank to the sound of sad movies and faded dreams.

Bitter like the taste of poison in my veins.

Once, you were the tender kiss of morning coffee upon my lips, the gentle warmth of the sun as it streamed through worn blinds and washed over our bones, our limbs tangled in the bed we used to share.

Now, there is only the imprint of your memory, laid to rest in the cold grave next to me where you belong no more.

Yet still you remain, trapped inside my heart where the acidity of all we became seeps into my bloodstream and contaminates my flesh, my organs, my soul.

Yet still you remain, trapped inside the walls of my unforgiveness, where I have refused to set you free. Where I have imprisoned you to my hatred, to make you suffer the wrath of my anger the way I had to suffer yours.

Except the only person who suffers is me.

I step outside, barefoot, and feel the cool of grass between my toes. The air is fresh and pure, and I breathe it into my lungs, ache for it to cleanse the remnants of you that reside within my core.

No longer do I wish to keep you here inside my

heart, where you corrode my veins. No longer do I wish to keep you here, where I am shackled to pain, where I am captive to misery with every breath I take.

I gaze at the horizon where city meets sky, and in this moment I know.

There is nothing to do but forgive you.

There is no weakness in forgiving you; it is not an ill-fought surrender.

It is bravery, it is strength. It is release, liberation; freedom.

It is an act of love.

Not only in setting you free,

But in setting myself free.

Because in forgiving you, I forgive me.

I forgive the girl who needed to be loved whatever the cost, no matter how much it hurt. Who didn't understand back then how much she was worth and all that she deserved. Who settled for less, settled for abuse, turned the other cheek—all in the name of love.

I forgive the girl who made mistakes, who made wrong choices, who hurt other people because of how much she was hurting. I forgive her that she stayed when she should have walked away. I forgive her vulnerability, her weakness, her desperate need for acceptance. I forgive her that she didn't know how to fight for her heart back then.

But now she does.

Three simple words.

I forgive you.

No longer will I continue to hurt you for the way you hurt me.

But more important, no longer will I continue to hurt myself.

I step back inside, get dressed, and make myself some coffee. The day stretches out before me like any other.

Nothing has changed, except, everything has.

Finally, I am free.

On Learning to
Love Again

Drought-Stricken Love

And I have seen what love does,
Razor blades against soft flesh.
Blood poured like mulled wine
into glasses that get shattered
against walls of hurt and blame.
I pay no heed to the rising thirst
that wells from beneath my skin.
I am dry bones, dust-filled veins,
arid landscapes of wasted hope.
Here, there is nothing left in me
that can bleed upon the ground.
Here, there is nowhere love can
grow in this drought soul of mine.
But still, even without the rains,
a flower will bloom in the desert,
and I cannot help but pick petals
that break through parched soil.
They are blown into the distance,
and the echo of my hopeful voice
is carried upon the summer winds.
He loves me, he loves me not.

How to Love the Woman Who Has Been to Hell and Back

The woman who has been to hell and back is not easy to love.

Many have tried. Most have failed.

The weak need not attempt, for it will take more strength than you even know you possess, more patience, more resilience, more tenacity, more resolve. It requires a relentless love that is determined and not easily defeated.

The woman who has been to hell and back will push you away. She will test you in her desire to know what you are made of, whether you have what it takes to weather her storm. Because she is unpredictable—at times a hurricane, a force of nature that rides on the fury of her suffering; at other times a gentle rain, calm, still, and quiet.

When she is the gentle rain that falls in time to her silent tears, love her.

When she is the thunder and lightning and ferocious winds that wreak havoc, love her harder.

She is a contradiction, a pendulum that will forever swing between fear of suffocation and fear of abandonment, and even she will not know how to find the balance between the two. Because today, although she will never tell you, she will feel insecure. She will want you to stay close, tuck her hair behind her ear, kiss her on her forehead, and hold her in the strength of your arms. But tomorrow she will crave her independence, her space, her solitude.

For while you have slept, she has been awake, unable to slow her thoughts, watching clocks and chasing time, trying to make the broken pieces fit, to make sense of it all—of where and how she fits. She fights her demons and slays her dragons, afraid if she goes to sleep, they will gain the upper hand; afraid if she goes to sleep, she will no longer be in control. Tomorrow she will be tired, and your presence will smother her. She will need only herself.

When she reaches out to you, love her.

When she pushes you away, lover her harder.

New situations and places and people and experiences will make her anxious. She will be fiercely independent and long to overcome her fears, all the while as terrified as a small child alone in the big world. Sometimes she will need to be courageous, to prove to herself she has what it takes. Other times she will need you to take her hand and hold it firmly in yours. Sometimes she may not know what she needs, and you will need to read her like a book with worn pages and a tattered spine, and be what she needs when she does not know herself.

When she is brave and steps into the world on her own, love her.

When she is scared but refuses to take your hand, love her harder.

She will live in fear of not being enough and always being too much—an endless battle to find the middle ground. Ashamed if the scale falls one way or the other, ashamed to be herself, because no one has ever loved her both when she is small and also when she is tremendous.

When she feels too much, love her.

When she feels not enough, love her harder.

Sometimes she won't hurt, the light will shine from her eyes, and her laughter will be a rare and precious melody. But sometimes she will hurt so much from the trauma still in her body that she will ache, she will feel pain and anguish. The light will grow dim, and the music will fade.

When she is the light, love her.

When she is the darkness, love her harder.

She will always love you with caution, with one foot out the door. For she does not understand a love with no conditions, one that is powerful enough to withstand hard times. She cannot allow herself to fully trust in your love, and she will keep parts of her heart hidden— the parts that have been hurt the most, the parts she can't risk being hurt again when she has worked so hard to stitch them together.

She will always watch, wait, and expect you to leave first. And when you don't, she has a truth written upon her heart that says you will—it's only a matter of time, because everyone who loves her leaves her. And so she will seek to sabotage the relationship, she will seek to destroy it, she will seek to leave first, she will seek to hurt you before you can hurt her. This is how she stays in control, how she survives, how she will ensure she will not get hurt again.

When she wants to love you, love her.

When she wants to hurt you, love her harder.

Being out of control terrifies her. Don't ever make her feel powerless, trapped, or without her freedom. She needs to dance barefoot under enormous blue skies, to feel sand between her toes, to run with wolves as the wind weaves magic through her hair, for here is where her healing is found. Never clip her wings, for if she has the freedom to fly, she will always come back to you.

Love her when it's easy, and love her harder when it's not.

Love her in a way that will defy all she has ever known love to be.

Love her because you understand with every fibre of your soul, the gift of her love, what it has cost her to offer you her fragile heart.

She does not need you. She has chosen you.

Because you have what it takes to survive the storm.

Because even when she doesn't know how to love, you know how to love harder.

Surrender

There is a need to be safe.

But there is a greater need to be loved.

We are warriors who have fought hard,

Survivors who have only known the battle.

But somehow, we must become

Courageous humans

Who embrace the surrender.

We must find a way to lay down

Our defences and surrender

Our weapons of self-preservation.

For we have battled long enough

In our solitude.

We know how to stay safe.

We know how to survive.

But now, dear heart,

We must know how to live.

Lay Me Bare

Lay me bare,

Pull back my layers,

And see all I hide beneath.

Lay me bare,

Force away the surface

Of my pretence,

Expose me.

Expose the parts of me I conceal.

Excavate through the rubble

Of my make-believe.

Find the truth I leave unseen.

Lay me bare,

Rip away my skin,

Tear away my flesh.

Reach into my bones,

Into the marrow that lies within.

See it. Touch it. Feel it.

For it is not pretty, but it is real,

And beauty deceives

While flesh and bone cannot lie.

Lay me bare,

Hear all I do not say,

And all I say but do not mean.

Strip me down and see my fears,

See my pain,

See beyond my subterfuge.

Lay me bare

Until all that remains

Is everything I am afraid to reveal.

And then lay your flesh

Next to my flesh,

And let us love the bare bones

Of one another's soul

In the wakefulness

Of this moment.

I'm Sorry I'm Not Easier to Love

I'm sorry that I'm not easier to love,
That I am made of barbed wire fences
And walls crowned with razor wire.
There is blood all over your fingers;
You are a true warrior, determined.
I admire your courage to continue
Even though you are ripped apart
By the piercing of my cold silence.
I long to let down my sharp edges
But my skin has already been torn,
And I'm scared to cut myself open
To allow you to step closer to me.
For I have sewn the bloody hands
Of everyone who has come before,
Who thank me that I mended them,
Then watch me bleed until I die.

There is nothing simple about loving the girl with the guarded heart.

She is not convinced by flowers and fancy dinners, nor won over by compliments and praise. In the beginning, she is a slow dance, one step towards you, another step back, as she learns to trust the ways of your heart and the strength of your arms. The dance may be slow, but it cannot be rushed, for she will sense the impatience of your steps and the way they fall out of time with hers. Dance with her. Follow the measure of her steps, and in time she will soon look to follow yours.

She will not show you her heart all at once, instead offering you a little at a time, unhurried and watchful of the way you hold each fragile piece. She longs for you to understand how much it takes her to show you these pieces, for you to trace your fingers over the scars left behind from others, for you to feel the whisper of your breath against her neck as you promise to hold her heart with more care than those who came before. There are parts of her heart that remain unreachable, parts she has buried under layers she will never reveal. Love these parts of her, the parts unseen, the shadows of her soul. For even the sky knows without darkness, the stars cannot adorn us with their light.

She will watch you closer than you realize, listen to every word you speak, and weigh it against every action, searching for inconsistencies and seeking the truth of your word and the intentions of your heart. Not because she can't trust you, but because she is cautious, alert, and wary; the stories of her past still etched upon her mind. She isn't ready to trust her heart with you. Not yet. Not until she knows you are a man of your word, a man of steadfast hands and unchanging ways.

There is a part of her that will always remain a little detached, ready to run, if she thinks her heart will get damaged again. She no longer believes in second chances, having used all of them on those undeserving of such grace. To hurt her means to lose her, for she would sooner be alone than risk losing the life she has fought so damned hard to rebuild with her own wearied hands. She isn't there because she needs you. She doesn't need anyone. She's there because she has chosen you, because she wants you, because she believes you are worth the risk. And all she asks is for you not to prove her wrong in the chance she has taken, for it has cost her more than you know.

She will need more reassurance than most. She will need you to stay present, available, and mindful of her scars. She will think too much, talk too little, cry too often, ask too many questions, and struggle to rest in your love.

She is complex. Complicated. Perplexing. Sometimes difficult.

But beyond her guarded heart lies a soul that contains the wonders of the universe. One that longs to live and love with abandon, that desires connection and intimacy and to be in relationship with someone who sees both her beauty and her scars, and knows how to fall in love with both.

She holds within her a fierce spirit: brave, strong, courageous, unrelenting. Yet it is also the quiet and the calm, a place to take shelter against the fury of the wind on storm-filled days. She is nurture, she is passion. She is a touch of madness against ordinary skies, a vulnerable heart with a fearless soul, a barefoot warrior who follows no trails but sets her own path.

She is grounded in her truth, accepting of her flaws, far from perfect but closer to real than most. She is wildflowers and ocean currents and meadows that dance upon the breath of summer winds, uncontained in earthly beauty and free in spiritual grace.

Broken, she knows what it means to suffer. But out of the depths of her suffering, she has come to understand love. And her guarded heart waits for the one who understands it too.

No, there may be nothing simple about loving the girl with the guarded heart.

But every day you choose to love her, she'll prove to you why she's worth it.

Homesick

Come closer, my love.

Distance frays my perspective,

And I cannot see for the miles

That stand between you and I.

You tell me you love me,

But I am tired of words

For I have heard of love before

From the mouth of boys

Who used words to fill gaps

That exist in their hollow hearts.

Come closer, my love.

Let me taste your truth

In the urgency of your kiss,

Feel honesty in the grip

Of your hands upon my flesh,

Hear sincerity in the quickening

Of your breath against my neck.

For I am terrified of tomorrow,

Should I wake to discover

It was never the miles

That separated me from you,

But the distance you placed

Between your heart and mine.

Come closer, my love,

For tonight I wander, lost,

And words are not enough

For me to find my way home

In you.

"I'm afraid of love. My heart has only ever slipped through the fingers of foolish boys with careless hands," she said.

And then she looked down at the dirt engraved on his hands and saw he too was a warrior. And in that moment, she knew the blood-stained hands of a man who had fought many battles would hold her heart with more care than a boy too afraid to get dirt on his hands ever could.

And It Is Not Love I Want Inside My Veins

And it is not love I want inside my veins.

I'd rather saltwater seep under my skin

From oceans that fill my lonely dreams.

For I am made of water, and love of oil.

I have seen how their molecules resist

And repel against one another's being;

They pull away from each other, bitter—

The only way I've known love to taste.

No, I do not want love with all its agony.

I would rather be drowned by the ocean

Than to have love flow through my veins,

Where I'll crave it the way I crave poetry

And red wine and the warmth of my bed.

But still, your eyes are clear and in them

I see the same oceans of which I dream.

You are tides that pull my mouth to you.

The taste of saltwater sits upon your lips,

And I know it streams through your veins

The same way that it does through mine.
We are water, both hydrogen and oxygen.
I long to resist the way I am drawn to you,
But we are molecules attracted by forces
That cause my heart to betray its resolve.
I tell you I don't want love inside my veins,
But I tattoo your name inside my forearm
And watch the letters bleed under my skin,
And we both know my tongue speaks lies.

Salty tears fall in straight lines
And create an ocean at my feet.
He says he's worried I'll drown
Beneath this flood of heartache.
I tell him no, for though I'm tired,
I will not drown, for I have learnt
To tread the waters of my sorrow.
He closes his body around mine
And lifts me into his strong arms.
With stable hands, he carries me
And lays me down upon dry land.
Through him, I learn of surrender.
Through him, I learn I am safe.

We Build Bridges Across the Ravine

You saw the ravine that was my heart

But you did not fear the broken ground,

Unlike the ones who came before

With their cautious feet

And feeble constitution.

You are braver than most,

You do not tiptoe around

These uncertain pathways.

Instead, you seek them out,

Tread with purpose, intention,

Though all too aware of the fall.

I wait for you to lose courage,

To turn and trace your steps back

To places that do not falter.

But you are not of faint heart

As you make your way down

Into the deepest crevice you can find.

You are not fearful of the dark,

Nor are you fearful of the thorns

That could well afflict your side.

Your hands graze the rough edges,

And I am made less abrasive.

Your lips taste the hollow pain,

And my flesh is no longer abandoned.

You are strong in the places I hurt.

You are not afraid of the cracks in my heart;

I am not afraid of the cracks in yours.

Together we build bridges.

Together we heal.

I Wish I Could Be Better for You

I wish I could be better for you,
That I could be like the poems
You read when you can't sleep.
Like the first taste of red wine
That kisses your eager mouth,
Or the drops of saltwater that
Cling to your skin on a hot day.
I wish your fingers didn't bleed
From holding on so tight to me,
That your ribs were not broken
From the way you fit my heart
Inside the safety of your chest.
I wish I was more than sadness,
That I could be louder than my
Silence and softer than my rage.
I wish I had been taught of love—
The love you are well taught in,
Not the kind of love that forces
Your legs open in the night-time
And fills your mouth with shame.

I wish I was not made of mistrust

And sewn together with betrayal.

Maybe then I would know how to

Be like the woman in your poems.

Maybe then I would know how to

Be better for you.

Your Mess Is Mine

"Bring me to your house
Tell me, sorry for the mess
Hey I don't mind
You're talking in your sleep
Out of time
Well, you still make sense to me
Your mess is mine." —Vance Joy

There are days our hearts are ripped open in our chests, and we cannot stop the blood as it splashes on the pristine walls around us and spills on the unsullied ground at our feet.

Sorry for the mess. Sorry for the mess. Sorry for the mess.

Days where chaos overwhelms us, sends us out of control; hurricane-force winds that leave all within our path upturned, strewn, dazed in the wake of our madness.

Sorry for the mess. Sorry for the mess. Sorry for the mess.

Days we are an ocean, tumultuous, unpredictable; the volume of our tears and the breath of our fury creates a tsunami, and we smash down on those around us, flood them with our rage, with our temper, with our despair.

Sorry for the mess. Sorry for the mess. Sorry for the mess.

There is nothing pretty about our hearts when they are ripped open and exposed. There is nothing pretty about our pain and grief and suffering as they spill onto the ground. There is nothing pretty about our contorted faces as we lay curled on the floor, soaked in our own tears.

There is nothing pretty about abandonment, rejection, brokenness, jealousy, maliciousness, hate. Nothing pretty about being sliced open by ourselves, by others, by trauma, abuse, memories, nightmares, triggers, and words as sharp as knife blades. There is nothing pretty about love—so often that which makes us bleed the most.

Sorry for the mess. Sorry for the mess. Sorry for the mess.

We are so ashamed of our mess, terrified to let anyone see it. We wipe off the filth, the scum, the stains, and only show up for the world when we are clean and presentable. We are loath to make others uncomfortable. To see them look away. To see them leave before they are asked to help clean the blood off the walls.

Before they are confronted with our humanity.

We've been told not to cry, to be quiet, not to make a scene, to hide our feelings.

We've been told not to make a mess.

Sorry for the mess. Sorry for the mess. Sorry for the mess.

But to be human is to be messy.

And the most beautiful gift we can give others is to step into their messiest place and say, "Hey, I don't mind." To look around at their mess, their chaos, the blood, and to make sense of them when they can no longer make sense of themselves. To sit with them in their mess, be comfortable in the disarray, wipe the blood from the walls and the shame from their hearts.

To embrace their humanity as our own.

To hear them say it:

Sorry for the mess. Sorry for the mess. Sorry for the mess.

And to love them enough to say, "Your mess is mine."

Give Me All Your Broken Pieces

Give me all your broken pieces,
And I will use them to build us
A house down near the ocean,
Where the sound of the waves
Will hush your demons to sleep.
A house with an open fireplace
Which will burn against the cold
That has forged into your bones.
I will make sure the windows are
Bigger and taller than we are so
The light will fall in straight lines
Upon the shadows of your face.
I will build us a house where the
Bed will always be warm, and the
Smell of coffee as you wake will
Mingle with salt air on your skin.
And in the evenings, you will sit
In your favourite chair, and I will
Pour you wine and read poems
That will sound like our prayers,
And the words will be like balm
That soothes your aching heart.

And if your broken pieces were
To become so sharp my fingers
Begin to bleed, then I will write
Blood-stained words along the
Doorpost of our house that say,
"You are loved," and if you ever
Find yourself lost, I will leave the
Porch light on, and you will walk
Up the steps and read my words.
And you will know you have found
Your way home.

Gravity

And we pretended not to notice

The way we were drawn to one another,

As if we could deny the force of our attraction

Any more than the stars could deny

The way they were forever pulled into the arms

Of the evening sky.

I Love You in the Spaces

I love you in the spaces,

In the pause between breaths,

The lull between seconds,

The falter between heartbeats.

In hushed quietness,

In sacred darkness.

The place where the universe

Whispers her secrets

To the dreamers and storytellers,

The poets and music makers.

She asks me to whisper mine,

And it is your name I breathe.

For it is you who fills the spaces

That exist between time.

There I will love you in silence

There I will love you unseen.

Meet Me on Roads Less Travelled

Meet me not on roads

Already gone before,

But find me where

The bridal creeper

Tangles its stem

Around fallen limbs,

And the sun

Scarcely dapples light

Through the dense canopy

Of leaves that surround

With their secrets untold.

Where above and below,

The heavens echo

With the same cry

Our hearts make

As they beat wild inside

Our drunken chests.

Take my hand in yours

And run with me, my love,

So even the wind

In all her delicate fury

Cannot compare to the breath

Inside our eager lungs.

Let us laugh

And kiss

With careless abandon

As we run along tracks

Dense with bracken and weed,

Where ground is untouched

And our spirits are untamed.

Let us not be like them,

For you and I do not belong

On well-worn trails

And familiar paths.

We are born of dust and skies,

Of constellation and earth.

And the purpose that aches

Inside our unbridled veins

Will lead us together

Along the road less travelled

To the place

Where freedom is found.

We Are Ropes Entwined in Sheets

We are ropes, entwined in sheets.

He tangles limbs around my body;

I untangle knots within his soul.

I am frayed, and he is splintered.

We lie, twisted and unkempt,

A mess of matted confusion.

His fingers trail my worn lines;

My hands graze his rough edges.

We are unravelled, yet healed,

Strands of chaos and repair.

He is abrasive upon my lips;

I am coarse beneath his touch.

We are broken complexities

Held together by flawed thread,

Delicate yet beautifully wild,

Woven flesh in perfect texture.

Unspoken Words

In darkness we wrote words we could never speak

On pages that wept with the stain
of our bleeding hearts,

Only to surrender our desires to the truth of the day

In the same way stars surrender their
light to the morning sky:

Silently,

Sorrowfully,

With yearning for the night carved upon their souls.

I Want You to Wake with Me

I want you to wake with me

In the place where salt air

Floats through our open window

And soaks into our thirsty skin.

The place where our minds

Are as tangled together

As our bodies

Beneath the worn sheets.

Where I find refuge in

The tremble of your breath

Against mine.

I want you to wake with me

In the place where clocks

Do not exist, and time

Steals naught away.

The place where fear

Loses grip on my heart

With each moment

Your ravenous hands

Take grip of my flesh,

No longer falling away

But complete.

I want you to wake with me

In the place where the pieces

Of our glorious madness

At once make perfect sense.

The place where you

Will trace gentle lines

Over the scars I hide.

And I will kiss healing

Into the wounds you deny,

And our skin will weep

No more.

I want you to wake with me

In the place we will never leave,

And here we will make our home,

Here we will stay.

Charcoal Hearts

I am bruised shades
Of dark grey and black.
Like a charcoal drawing,
I smear and I smudge
Outside of the lines
They draw around me.
Your fingers touch me,
And I stain their beauty.
"I'm sorry," I whisper
As I wash the blemish
From your pure hands
With my broken tears.
"Stop," you murmur
As you pull me closer,
Your skin now tainted
With the same shade
Of darkness as on me.
We are wondrous art
Stained upon canvas,
My burden now yours,
Your heart now mine.

Let Me Love You When You've Forgotten How to Love Yourself

Lay your body down next to mine.

Let me trace my fingertips along

The hidden map of your sadness,

Where I will search for the places

You have buried your pain beneath

The fault lines on your jagged skin.

For I am not of faint heart, or afraid

To fall deeply into your brokenness.

I am not scared to reach my hands

Into the space of your hollow bones

And unearth your shielded darkness.

I will not be crushed below the weight

Of the sorrow that closes your lungs;

Instead, I will place it upon my chest.

For today I am strong, and I will carry

The heaviness that your heart cannot

Let me wash your wounds with tears

And bandage your grazes with kisses.

Let me tangle my body around yours,
My warmth a blanket while you sleep.
Let me heal you with love when you
Have forgotten how to love yourself.

And he was the first

To understand me,

For he traced his fingers

Along my scars

And read them like stories,

Knowing they would speak

More truth

Than words ever could.

On Finding the
Courage to Rise

Free

And she thought

To be accepted,

She had to be good.

Follow the rules.

Do everything right.

Be perfect.

Keep them comfortable.

But good wasn't real,

And she began to shrink

Inside the lies of who

She pretended to be

Until she became

So small her bones

Crushed inside her frame

And she broke wide open,

Scattered pieces laid bare

For the world to see.

A glorious destruction.

No longer hidden.

All of her naked.

Uncovered. Bleeding.

Exposed.

Free.

Real lost her many things.

But her soul it found.

And she would rather

Walk alone in her

Wondrous truth than

Forfeit her *real*

For a scrap of their

Shallow acceptance.

Courage to Fly

You gaze with longing at forget-me-not skies while you remain grounded on the earth below, so deeply rooted in your fear. Fear of rejection, fear of failure, fear of others. Afraid to fall, yet even more afraid to fly. You fear success as much as you fear defeat, and so you tell yourself you are content here on familiar land where it is comfortable, safe. Yet your spirit is a restless wind, a fervent ocean, like a force of nature; your heart is wild, free, uncontained.

Beloved, you have been held down for so long now. The weight of all you have carried corrupted your wings until you no longer tried to fly—worse yet, until you no longer wanted to. And now, even as you heal, even as you are healed, you are too afraid to once again lift your wings towards skies that long to set you free.

But look at all you have become. See your strength, resilience, power, beauty, determination, fortitude. Now is your time to take flight beloved. The universe is quiet, hushed, as it waits with eager anticipation to see you rise, to stand in awe of your creation just as it did the day you were born.

Everything you need is contained within your valiant spirit. You are light to the darkest of places, salt to the corners of the earth, healing to the wounded, love to the broken-hearted.

Your faith wavers, so fragile in your chest, so unsure, so filled with doubt. Breathe, for you no longer have spirit of fear, but a spirit of power. Your heart can no longer be contained in your chest, your spirit no longer caged in your body, your wings no longer cast down by your side.

All you need now, beloved, is the courage to fly.

She Will Be the Storm

And no longer will she exist

To keep you comfortable.

She is not here to play small,

To shrink her bones inside

Your walls of expectation,

To lower her voice alongside

Your hushed disapproval,

To hide her strength to

Appease your weak inadequacy.

No, she will be the sky

Abundant in endless dimension;

The thunder, ferocious as it trembles;

The heart of mountains;

The wind, unstoppable in its rampage

Through barren field and city street.

She will be the storm:

Loud, wild, unapologetic,

No longer silent in her truth.

It Was Not My Freedom You Feared but Your Own

I will hurl expectation to the ocean
of burden you drown beneath.

I will untie my hands from the duty
you enslave your heart to.

I will dance upon the grave of the
buried obligation you die below.

I will howl truths upon the mountains
you lack courage to tread.

I will sprint breathless towards the
deliverance you turn away from.

I will tear apart the walls of the
prison you call protection.

I will revel in the abundance of
the life you deny yourself,

The life you denied me.

For I understand now it was not
my freedom you so feared,

But your own.

I Wonder if You Knew You Saved Me

I wonder if you knew back then
That grief would have a name,
And it would taste like me:
Bitter, like the dregs
Of pitch-black coffee
I left upon your lips.

I wonder if you knew back then
That you would have to bury
Me in the splintered coffin
Built inside your mind,
Knowing I carry heartbeat
Still, just no longer yours.

I wonder if you knew back then
That ghosts are not people,
But memories that stain,
Endless, like faded nicotine
Under cracked fingers,
Never scrubbed away.

I wonder if you knew back then
Of the sound loneliness makes,
The hollow scratching that
Claws inside your chest,
Tearing flesh from bone
And me from you.

I wonder if you knew back then
That I was made from the grit
Woven through tangled earth
And the salt flung across
Tempestuous ocean,
Wild and unafraid.

I wonder if you could've known
Of all you would come to lose
The day my worth was found.
I wonder if you will ever know
You did not break me, my love –
You saved me.

Hush Now

Hush now, your emotions are bleeding all over the floor.

Ashamed, you pick them up and force
them back inside your chest.

You are too much; they turn their face away, and
you cover your naked soul, apologetic. You are too
loud, too honest, too passionate, too sorrowful,
too messy. Too much feeling. Too much real.

Once again you shrink yourself inside their cage
because you think it's better to fit within their
expectations than feel the pain of their rejection.

Darling, don't.

You don't belong in their cage.

A heart as big and wild and brave and valiant
as yours was never meant to be tamed.

Never let anyone silence your voice.

Never let anyone smother your wild.

Never let anyone have the power to
make you believe you are *too much.*

For you are not too much.

It is they who will never be enough to
comprehend the greatness of all that you are.

Raison d'Etre

It's not the silence you fear,
But the sound of your own heart
As it beats purpose into your veins
And calling into your soul.
You are not afraid of inadequacy,
But of greatness, for this you feel
You are not worthy to carry.
Hushed, you do not breathe,
Scared to give life to the spark
That will set your spirit alight,
Uncontrollable, unstoppable.
But dear heart, can you not see?
The world lies cold in its apathy,
Longing for the heat of a wildfire
To bring it back to life.

The Hero of the Story

The story you wrote on her heart was abandonment,

But in the silence of your departure,
she would come to know

She had the power to rewrite the ending,

And the only hero she had ever needed

Was herself.

Inadequate

And they will always try to make you feel inadequate.

They will grab you by the hand, drag you down your alleyway of imperfections, and show you the walls lined with your failures. They will claw their hands deep inside the pit of your stomach, search out your insecurities, and place them behind your eyelids where, even in sleep, there will be no escape from your deepest fear of scarcity. They will barrage your mind with taunted whispers of all you should be, with ridicules of all you are not. They will wear down the resistance of your heart with arrows of rejection and dismissal and ostracism and abandonment for every moment you attempt to stand firm upon the truth of your own heart.

This is how they crush your bones so you fit inside their box, where they will always be able to shape you into who they want you to be.

This is how they throw a blanket on your fire, until your flames are no more and you become only the ashes and dust of who you were created to be.

This is how they wrap their cords around your throat, until your skin is raw and the power of your voice is silenced by the fear of speaking out loud.

This is how they keep you small. This is how they keep you quiet.

This is how they keep you from being more than they will ever be.

And when they have almost succeeded, and you have forgotten the sound of your own name, let me remind you, my love.

Let me remind you that you have been created beyond compare. That every breath you take is the heartbeat of an answered prayer. You are perfect in your flaws, made more beautiful by the broken pieces you stitched together with your threads of courage and hope, threads that glimmer in the sunlight and warm the darkest shadows of those around you. You are a heart made of soft wool that wraps its compassion around others when the world gets too cold for them. You are the strength and resilience of an oak tree that others clamber beneath when the wind blows and the storm rages. You are the force of the night as it triumphs over the day, the softness of the tide as it surrenders to the moon. You are incomparable fingerprints and remarkable thoughts imminent inside the beauty of your mind. Your eyes are colours of marbles not yet named, and your laughter is made of music never heard before, and your toes beckon upon winded paths not yet imprinted by others.

They will always try to make you feel inadequate.

And some days you will believe them. You will believe you are nothing more than the mistakes you live to regret, nothing more than the times you have failed, fallen short, the sum of your deficiencies. You will believe you are only deserving of love and acceptance if you comply, conform, make yourself *less than* so you do not overshadow or intimidate or threaten them with the fury of your flames. But you are born of the galaxies and made from the fire of the stars they contain.

You are here to burn for all that sets your heart on fire and watch it turn to gold.

They will always try to make you feel inadequate.

Don't let them. Listen for the sound of your own name. For here lies everything you are. Everything they are afraid of. Everything they will never be.

And everything the world is waiting for.

Transformation

And you, with your autumn soul,

Tears that fall with the silence

Of dead leaves

As they dance to the ground.

Your heart changes colour,

Gold and crimson shades

Of melancholy

Against skies of marbled ink.

Winter is approaching.

You fear its hand of destruction,

Afraid of its merciless cold.

But dear heart,

You have never seen

The beauty in loss,

In letting go,

In surrender.

So strip to the bare

Splendour of your bones.

Allow the bitter kiss of death

To steal what must remain no more.

For only in the sorrow of our demise

Will we come to understand

The power in our transformation.

Destiny

She is a wave,

And you are the ocean

Who longs to hold her back from the shore.

But she can no more be contained

From her destiny than falling stars

Can be contained

In the midnight sky.

Someone You Used to Know

You speak the broken pain of regret
Into the place you laid my memory.
The sound echoes then fades away—
Remorse lost inside an empty grave.
Yours were the words that killed me,
Each one a fatal wound to the heart.
And now you want to keep me here
In this place of sorrow and sadness.
You imagine me to be crushed bones
And withered flesh upon decayed soul,
As if without you I have only perished,
As if you could ever hold in your hands
The power of my life and resurrection.
No, darling, you will not find me there
In the place you buried my torn body
With your own blood-stained hands.
I will not hear your hollow repentance
As you grieve the woman who is gone.
For I no longer dwell inside your grave,
Nor do I lie in the walls of your coffin.
Instead, I mended my shattered bones
And stitched together my gaping heart.

I rebuilt the woman you sought to kill

Because you left me without a choice.

I am no longer dead in the wake of you.

My heart beats wild and true and fast.

The world will know my scarred beauty,

They will see the way I rise from ashes

And walk in the strength of my worth.

But to you, I will be a faded memory

Of someone you once used to know

But never again will.

Magic and Madness

She was magic and madness,
And the moon fell in love with the way
It could not tame the wild tides
That rose and fell
Inside her frenzied chest.

Unapologetic

I watch the ocean, the way her wild waves smash against one another, a furious collision, unapologetic, and I wonder why she is so angry today.

And then her fury settles, and she kisses the shoreline with gentle strength, and it occurs to me that she is not angry.

She is free.

She is a force of nature, untamed in both her beauty and her rage. She is delicate and wild, calm and fierce. She does not apologize for being too much, or fear she is not enough. She just is, in all her beauty and intensity. She just is all she has been created to be.

I listen to her heartbeat and hear her whisper her secrets to me. She tells me that I am born of the same creation. That in me lies the same heart, the same force, the same beauty.

Untameable. Unyielding. Unapologetic.

Sun warms my face, saltwater seeps into my pores, and my weary heart begins to find its way back.

I am one with the ocean, and I am her and she is me, and we are life.

Leave Me in the Wilderness

Leave me here in the wilderness.

Let me wander upon lost paths,

Where fallen limbs and bracken

Cause my feet to stumble astray

Deeper down the unknown roads

That lead me further into myself.

Let my soul become entangled

With ivy and creeper and vine

As it twines through damp forest

And twists around my sad anguish.

Let moss grow upon my shadows

Until sunlight warms my bitter grief.

Let me grope through darkness,

And my heart taste its sour wrath

As it unleashes, wild and savage,

Upon the fury of its torn injustice

Until there is only hushed silence

Broken by the weep of surrender.

Let my spirit be found crushed
In valleys of dust and drought.
Let me be consumed with thirst
As I wait upon winds of the earth
To breathe life into my dry bones
And mend me back to abundance.

Do not take my hand and lead me
From this journey I choose to abide,
But leave me here in the wilderness
Where, for now, I must live untamed.
For I am young and so very broken,
And there is still much to be learned.

Anticipation

You crushed your bones until they became dust,

So you would be lifeless enough for them to love you.

But it wasn't enough.

You shrunk your heart until it withered to nothing,

So you would be cold enough for them to love you.

But it wasn't enough.

You tore your body into insignificant pieces,

So you would be small enough for them to love you.

But it wasn't enough.

Stop, dear one.

It will never be enough.

You will always be too much for the narrow
hearts and minds of this world.

For your purpose was never designed to
be held inside such shallow grasp.

Gather yourself, beloved. Mend your bones and rise.

For even the galaxies concede they
cannot contain the enormity

Of your soul within their endless skies.

Listen now, and hear the universe
breathe with hushed anticipation

As it patiently waits for you to step
into the glorious abundance

Of all you were created to be.

The Reclaiming

For so long you have walked this journey
With the sting of thistles upon your feet
And the stab of thorns along your sides,
Believing you deserve to suffer the pain
For the pain you have caused to others.
Your skin weeps with sorrow and shame,
You tear your hair and gouge your eyes,
Yet it is still never enough to satiate the
Desperate thirst for your self-atonement.
Come now, dear heart; you have dwelled
Long enough here in this valley of grief.
Wipe away the ashes from your forehead
And remove the sackcloth from your body.
Come, and pull the weeds from the ground.
Come, and reclaim this land that is yours.

Acknowledgements

Paul, it would take a lifetime to thank you for all you have been and all that you are. Thank you for eighteen years, for every better and every worse, and for every day of this crazy life we have created together. To me, love will always look like a cup of coffee in bed each morning. "And love is when someone who even knows your scars, stays to kiss them."[1] I love you.

William, Ben, Aliandra, Hannah: There are no words I could write that would ever do justice to how proud I am of each one of you. Every day you delight and amaze me. I stand in awe of the people you have become. Thank you for being my biggest fans. Thank you for the ways you have changed me. Thank you for the ways you have saved me.

PK, how can I even begin to thank you for the countless hours you have spent collaborating[2], proofreading, editing, advising, and being the rational to my irrational? Thank you for your steadfast, your constant, your unwavering. I am so appreciative of every single way you have helped bring this book to life. Thank you for being the best friend a girl could ever ask for.

To those with messy hair and messier hearts, who run barefoot under abundant skies; those who have carried me, held me, and lifted me. My tribe: thank you.

---

[1] Benjamin Griss.

[2] *Fault Lines Upon Your Heart* and *Viking Funeral* collaborated with Paul Kohn.

To my readers: without you this book wouldn't exist. Thank you for your endless support and words of encouragement, and for allowing me a space to grow. I appreciate each and every one of you.

Lastly, thank you to the ones who tried to break me.

I am stronger now because of you.

About the Author

Writer. Poet. Survivor. Warrior. Word alchemist.

Kathy Parker is a lover of beautiful words and wide open spaces. She has a wild heart, a passionate soul, and a gentle spirit. She is a survivor of abuse and a sufferer of complex PTSD. Her greatest desire is to see all women empowered with the truth of their glorious worth.

She is a contributor for The Mighty, Thought Catalog, Truth Code, Lessons Learned in Life, and The Minds Journal. She also has writing published at Huffington Post Australia and Elephant Journal.

She is married to a farmer in the Limestone Coast of South Australia and is a mother to four astonishing children.

You can find Kathy at www.kathyparker.com.au.